Contents

Social Security in a nutshell

4   *A program that helps everyone*

6   *The benefit design*

8   *Social Security's financing problem*

10   *Only 2 ways to fix the problem*

12   *The need for a long-lasting fix*

How benefits could be cut

16   ✂ ① *Cut benefits across-the-board today*

18   ✂ ② *Raise the Full Retirement Age*

20   ✂ ③ *Freeze the purchasing power of benefits*

22   ✂ ④ *Cut benefits for higher earners*

24   ✂ ⑤ *Change the cost-of-living adjustment*

26   ✂ ⑥ *Do nothing (but cut benefits in 2033)*

How revenues could be raised

30   ✦ ① *Increase the payroll tax today*

32   ✦ ② *Raise the earnings cap*

34   ✦ ③ *Tax health insurance*

36   ✦ ④ *Transfer start-up costs to general revenues*

38   ✦ ⑤ *Raise the return on assets*

40   ✦ ⑥ *Do nothing (but raise taxes in 2033)*

What about individual accounts?

42   *By themselves, they don't fix the problem*

Time to fix the problem

46   *A lasting fix*

48   *How the proposals stack up*

50   *Three key questions*

52   *Explanations*

Social Security
in a nutshell

Social Security helps everyone. Our older parents and grandparents, who paid into the program while working, now get a check each month. So do their spouses, disabled workers, and the dependents of breadwinners who die. We and our spouses and children will also collect benefits when we grow old, become disabled, or die.

Social Security provides a basic income, not enough to maintain our standard of living. The average worker who retired at 65 in 2013 gets 41 percent of pre-retirement earnings— $18,500 a year. So most people need to supplement Social Security with employer pensions, 401(k)s, and individual savings.

Social Security benefits are adjusted to keep up with inflation. And the checks keep coming as long as we live. Other sources of income often dry up toward the end of life, when we are most vulnerable. Social Security thus provides 70 percent of the income of households headed by someone age 80 or over.

SOCIAL SECURITY PROVIDES:

70% of the income of households age 80 or over

The program covers all of us.

Benefits replace a portion of our earnings from work. The more we earn and pay in tax, the higher our benefits. Social Security also tries to assure Americans a basic income after a lifetime of work. Because low earners spend more of their income on necessities, the program replaces more of our earnings if we don't earn a lot.

We can claim benefits at any age between 62 and 70. We collect for more years if we claim at 62. But Social Security adjusts the annual amount to keep lifetime benefits much the same. Annual benefits are thus much lower if claimed at 62 and much higher if claimed at 70.

Social Security will replace less of our earnings going forward because

- We're raising the age when we can claim full benefits from 65 to 67.
- Medicare premiums, which are deducted from Social Security checks before they're sent out, will take a greater share of our benefits.
- More of our benefits will be subject to income tax.

By 2030, benefits for the average worker who claims at 65 will fall to 36 percent of earnings, and to 31 percent net of Medicare premiums and income taxes vs. 37 percent today.

65 ⤑ 67

BENEFIT CUTS

Full benefits will be available at 67, not 65. Medicare premiums and income taxes will also take bigger bites.

ANNUAL BENEFITS DEPEND ON HOW MUCH YOU EARN AND PAY IN TAX

	LOW EARNER	AVERAGE EARNER	HIGH EARNER
Annual earnings	$20,300	$45,100	$85,000
Social Security % of earnings replaced if claimed at **age 65**	56%	41%	30%
Annual benefits if claimed at **age 65** in 2013	$11,200	$18,500	$26,300

THEY ALSO DEPEND ON WHEN YOU CLAIM

Annual benefit if claimed in 2010, at **age 62** (2013 dollars)		$14,900	
Annual benefit if claimed in 2018, at **age 70** (2013 dollars)		26,200	

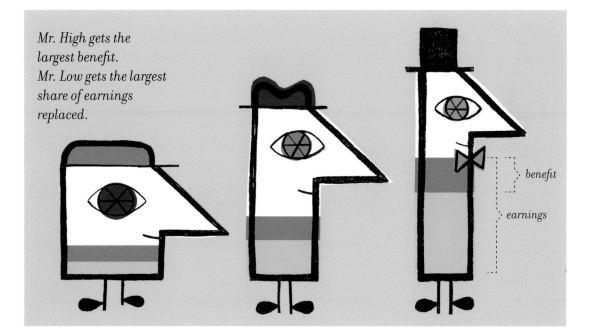

Mr. High gets the largest benefit. Mr. Low gets the largest share of earnings replaced.

benefit

earnings

Social Security has a financing problem.

Benefits are mainly financed by a 12.4 percent tax on earnings, split evenly between workers and employers. Far more of us, however, will soon be collecting benefits with not many more paying taxes.

2033:

The year Social Security will be able to pay only 77 cents on the dollar.

Until recently, not all of the 12.4 percent payroll tax was used to pay benefits. A portion was set aside in the Social Security Trust Fund, invested in government bonds, to help pay benefits down the road.

Since 2010, Social Security has needed to use interest income from the bonds to help pay benefits. Social Security could continue to pay benefits without raising the payroll tax if the bonds produced enough income.

In 2020, however, benefit costs will exceed Social Security's tax revenues and Trust Fund income. So the program will need to sell bonds to pay benefits.

In 2033, the Trust Fund will be depleted. Social Security will then be able to pay only 77 cents on the dollar. And the shortfall slowly widens thereafter.

- NOTE: Using Trust Fund interest and assets to pay benefits would not be a burden on the economy if the government used the Social Security surpluses it borrowed to pay down debt and increase national saving.

TODAY 3
WORKERS
CONTRIBUTE
FOR EACH
BENEFICIARY.

SOON THERE
WILL BE JUST 2.

THE TAXES
2 WORKERS
PAY WILL
NOT FINANCE
BENEFITS FOR 1
RETIREE

2013   2030

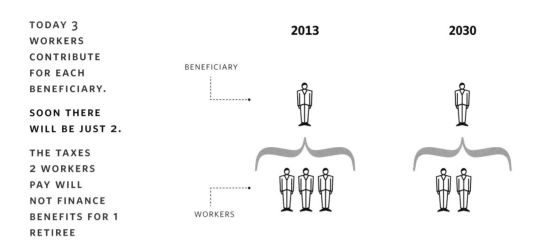

BENEFICIARY

WORKERS

AND BY 2033
THE TRUST
FUND WILL BE
EMPTY AND NO
LONGER ABLE
TO HELP PAY
BENEFITS

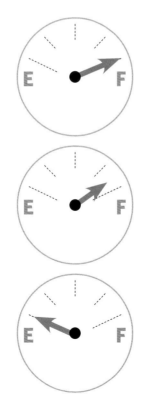

2010
Benefits greater than taxes
Need interest from bonds in the
Trust Fund to pay benefits

2020
Benefits greater than taxes + interest
Need to start selling bonds to
pay benefits

2033
Trust fund depleted

The only 2 ways to fix the problem are to cut benefits or increase revenues.

But cutting benefits is no walk in the park. And raising revenues is also tough.

Social Security benefits, which are hardly generous, are about the only source of income for a third of all elderly households. Another third gets more than half its income from the program.

The Social Security payroll tax is the largest tax most of us pay. It's especially burdensome on low-wage workers, who spend much of their earnings on necessities.

So it should come as no surprise that nothing has been done. But the longer we wait, the larger the benefit cut or tax increase needed to fix the problem.

HAS BEEN DONE

And the longer we dawdle, the harder the fix.

THE ELDERLY ARE HEAVILY DEPENDENT ON SOCIAL SECURITY

Social Security benefits as % of elderly household income

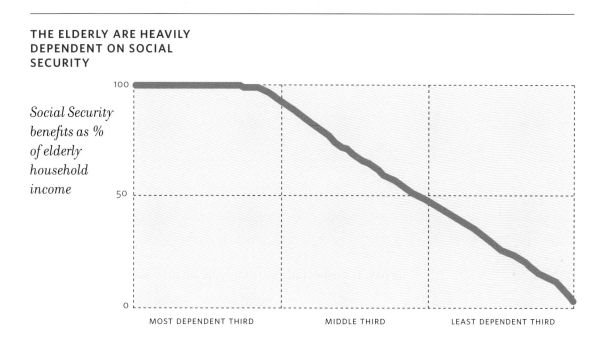

THE SOCIAL SECURITY PAYROLL TAX IS THE LARGEST TAX MOST OF US PAY

Federal taxes and credits as % of household income

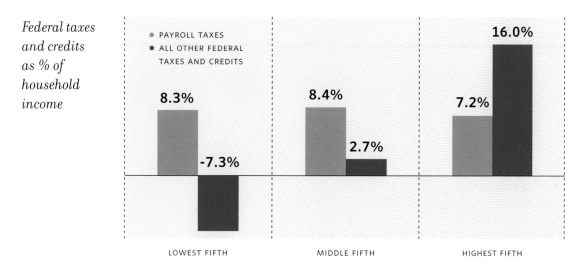

The fix should be long-lasting. Social Security uses a 75-year planning horizon, which sounds long-term. But a fix that only solves the problem for the next 75 years will typically build up assets in the near term and sell those assets to pay benefits at the end of the time frame. In the 76th year there are no more assets to sell. So the program falls off a cliff.

Solving the 75-year problem remains a reasonable place to start. But it's not a reasonable place to end. What follows are different ways to cut benefits or raise revenues, and the contribution each makes toward solving the 75-year shortfall. We then discuss what must be done to make a fix long-lasting.

REAL SECURITY

The fix should balance the books as far as the eye can see.

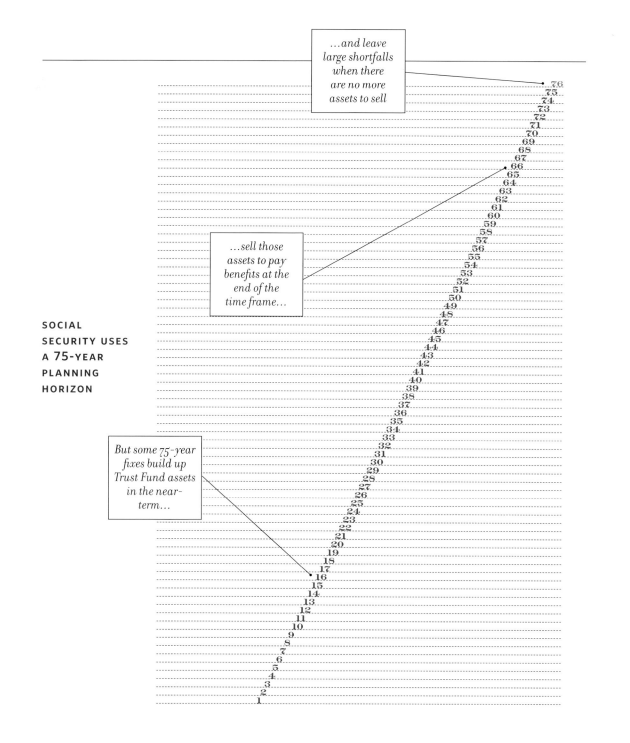

...and leave large shortfalls when there are no more assets to sell

...sell those assets to pay benefits at the end of the time frame...

SOCIAL SECURITY USES A 75-YEAR PLANNING HORIZON

But some 75-year fixes build up Trust Fund assets in the near-term...

How *benefits* could be *cut*

✂ Benefit cut 1

An immediate across-the-board cut

We could fix Social Security's financing problem over the program's 75-year planning horizon if we cut scheduled benefits by 17 percent for current and future beneficiaries. A portion of the payroll tax would then be sent to the Trust Fund. The payroll tax could also finance a greater share of the program's reduced obligations down the road. So the Trust Fund should last 75 years.

PROS	CONS
A 17 percent across-the-board benefit cut, for current and future beneficiaries, solves the 75-year financing problem.	This hits current beneficiaries, many with low incomes and no way to adapt, and could lead to an expansion of means-tested programs to assure a basic income.
It spreads the burden over all generations, including those currently collecting benefits.	Middle-income workers with inadequate 401(k)s would also be stressed.

NOT MY CHIMNEY!

A 17% across-the-board cut solves the problem for 75 years. But no politician has proposed cutting the benefits of today's retirees.

If we preserve the benefits of everyone 55 and over, as many suggest, the benefits of everyone younger must be cut more than 20%.

✂ Benefit cut 2

Raise the Full Retirement Age

The Full Retirement Age (FRA) is the age we can claim full benefits. If we claim earlier, annual benefits are less. The FRA is currently rising from 65 to 67. This means workers claiming at 65, or any age, will get less of their earnings replaced than in the past.

One proposal would continue to raise the FRA as lifespans increase, so that the portion of adult life over which we could collect full benefits stays the same.

PROS	CONS
Indexing the FRA to longevity cuts the 75-year shortfall by about 20 percent.	We must already work longer to offset the rise in the FRA and the increase in Medicare premiums and income taxes.
It recognizes that we probably need to work longer as we live longer.	Many who claim at 62 will have inadequate incomes later in life, as other sources of income dry up. So we might need to raise the earliest age one could claim, which would create hardship for some.

ANOTHER BIRTHDAY

Raising the FRA is reasonable if we are willing and able to work longer.
But it could create hardship at older ages if we continue to claim as early as we do today.

✂ Benefit cut 3

Freeze the purchasing power of benefits

Social Security benefits are designed to replace a portion of our earnings. As earnings and living standards have grown over time, so has the income Social Security provides.

We could end Social Security's earnings replacement function and freeze the purchasing power of benefits paid to future beneficiaries at current levels. Benefits would be able to buy the same goods and services as they do today. But as wages and living standards rise, they would support an ever-shrinking portion of our standard of living.

PROS	CONS
Freezing the purchasing power of benefits pretty much solves Social Security's financing problem.	The cuts are dramatic. Eventually, new beneficiaries get less than what the program could pay even after the Trust Fund is gone.
As benefit outlays fall below revenue inflows, Congress could lower the payroll tax or use the extra revenue to finance other programs.	Benefits in time could be seen as inadequate, and lead to a major expansion of means-tested welfare for the elderly.

LESS ON YOUR PLATE

Social Security would provide much less today had we frozen the purchasing power of benefits in the past.

Frozen benefits for the average earner who claims at 65

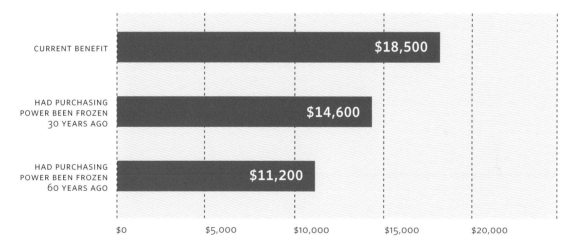

CURRENT BENEFIT	$18,500
HAD PURCHASING POWER BEEN FROZEN 30 YEARS AGO	$14,600
HAD PURCHASING POWER BEEN FROZEN 60 YEARS AGO	$11,200

$0 $5,000 $10,000 $15,000 $20,000

Low-wage workers who claim at 65 would get $6,800 a year had we frozen benefits 60 years ago.

✂ Benefit cut 4

Cut the benefits of higher earners

Cutting benefits across the board could reduce Social Security's guaranteed income for low earners below what's seen as minimally adequate.

An alternative is to shelter the benefits of low earners. One such proposal would continue to replace earnings as we do today for the bottom 30 percent of earners, freeze the purchasing power of the maximum benefit the program pays, and adjust all benefits in-between on a sliding scale.

PROS	CONS
Freezing benefits on a sliding scale cuts the 75-year shortfall by about 55 percent.	In time, all workers claiming at a given age would get much the same benefit, even though some had paid much more in tax.
Social Security would continue to provide a minimal basic income, limiting the need for means-tested welfare for the elderly.	This option sharply reduces Social Security's role in spreading income from one stage of life to another.

A BASIC STIPEND

Social Security would assure a minimally adequate income if we shelter low earners from benefit cuts.

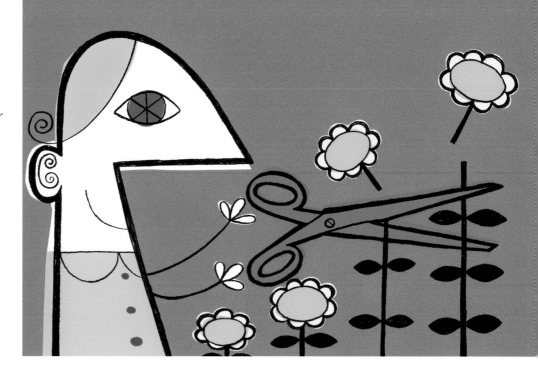

Benefits frozen on a sliding scale for **low**, **average**, and **high** earners who claim at age 65

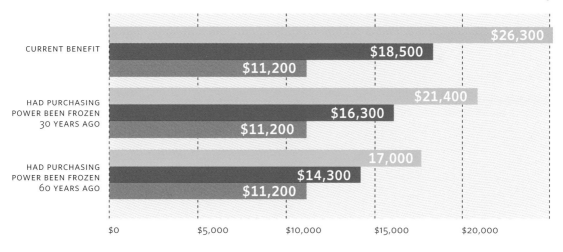

	low	average	high
CURRENT BENEFIT	$11,200	$18,500	$26,300
HAD PURCHASING POWER BEEN FROZEN 30 YEARS AGO	$11,200	$16,300	$21,400
HAD PURCHASING POWER BEEN FROZEN 60 YEARS AGO	$11,200	$14,300	17,000

✂ Benefit cut 5

Change the Cost-Of-Living Adjustment

Social Security provides annual Cost-Of-Living Adjustments to maintain the purchasing power of benefits. Economists generally agree, however, that the Consumer Price Index (CPI), which Social Security uses to measure inflation, rises faster than the prices most people actually pay. As we shift our spending from more expensive to less expensive items, the CPI doesn't fully reflect the changing mix of items we buy.

We could adopt a new measure of inflation to adjust benefits to changes in the cost of living.

PROS	CONS
Using a revised CPI cuts the 75-year shortfall by 20 percent.	Slowing benefit increases hits long-term beneficiaries—the disabled and the oldest old—who are least well-off and most dependent on Social Security.
If the revised CPI more accurately reflects changes in the cost of living, Social Security would work the way it's designed.	The disabled and the oldest old might not shift their spending very much, so the CPI might not overstate the increase in the prices they pay.

WHAT'S THE RIGHT ADJUSTMENT?

Lower COLAs would hurt the disabled and the oldest old, who are disproportionately poor.

✄ Benefit cut 6

Do nothing (but cut benefits in 2033)

We could do nothing—we're very good at that—and simply cut benefits in 2033 when the Trust Fund is depleted. If we cut across-the-board, including the benefits of those already disabled and retired, the program could then pay 77 cents on the dollar. The average worker who claims at 65 would get 28 percent of earnings—about $12,200 in terms of current wages—before reductions for Medicare premiums and income taxes. And if we shelter existing beneficiaries, new beneficiaries would get much less.

PROS	CONS
Cutting benefits to what taxes could pay when the Trust Fund is depleted solves the problem.	The cut is very deep and abrupt, and could impose significant hardship on those with low benefits and not much other income.
We don't have to do anything for 20 years.	This option could lead to a major expansion of means-tested welfare programs to assure minimally adequate incomes.

FUTURE SHOCK

Just cutting would slash the share of earnings the program replaces abruptly in 2033…

…*then slowly as rising longevity drives up costs.*

Earnings replacement for the average earner who claims at 65 (before reductions for Medicare premiums or income taxes)

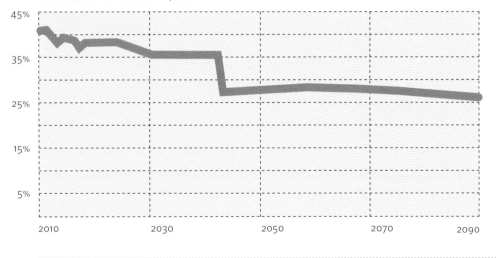

45%

35%

25%

15%

5%

2010   2030   2050   2070   2090

Benefits of the average worker who claims at 65,
in terms of current earnings, if we just cut benefits in 2033

2013	41%	$18,500
2030	36	$16,300
2033	28	$12,600

How *revenues* could be *raised*

⬆ Revenue increase 1

Increase the payroll tax rate today

We could fix Social Security's financing problem over the 75-year planning horizon if we raised the payroll tax by 2.9 percent of earnings, split between us and our employers. Social Security would build up a larger Trust Fund. The higher payroll tax could also finance a greater share of the program's obligations down the road. So the Trust Fund should last 75 years.

PROS	CONS
Increasing the payroll tax to 15.3 percent, split between us and our employers, solves the 75-year financing problem.	The increase could impose hardship on low-wage workers, who spend much of their income on necessities.

SIMPLEST FIX

A 2.9% increase in the payroll tax lets Social Security pay benefits for the next 75 years.

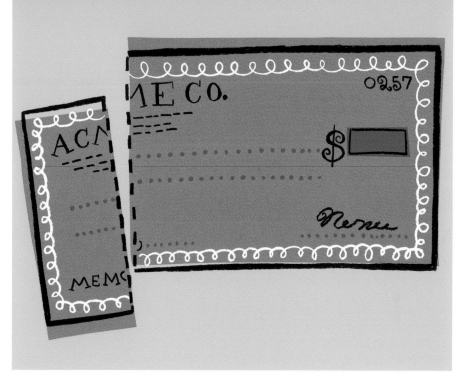

The trust fund would last 75 years
TRUST FUND AS PERCENT OF ANNUAL BENEFITS

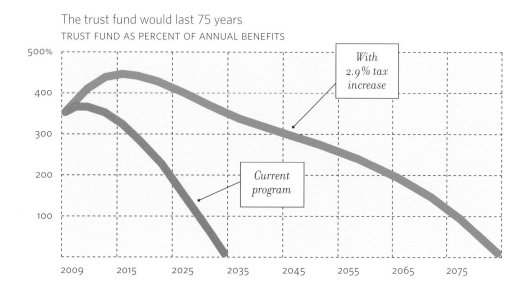

With 2.9% tax increase

Current program

500%
400
300
200
100

2009 2015 2025 2035 2045 2055 2065 2075

↑ Revenue increase 2

Raise the earnings cap

Social Security taxes and replaces earnings up to a certain level—$117,000 in 2014—with the earnings cap indexed to wage growth.

When the current cap was put in place, Social Security covered 90 percent of all U.S. earnings. But rising inequality pushed an increasing share of earnings above the ceiling, so Social Security now covers only 83 percent. One proposal would gradually reset the cap, over a 10-year period, to cover 90 percent of earnings.

PROS	CONS
Raising the earnings cap to cover 90 percent of earnings cuts the 75-year shortfall by about 30 percent.	Workers with earnings above the current cap would pay more in tax but not get much higher benefits in return.
It would affect workers who are relatively capable of bearing an increased burden— those making more than the current cap.	Raising the cap could undermine political support for the program among workers with the highest earnings.

TAX THE WELL-TO-DO
Raising the cap would only affect workers earning more than $117,000.

Distribution of full-time wage earners, 2012

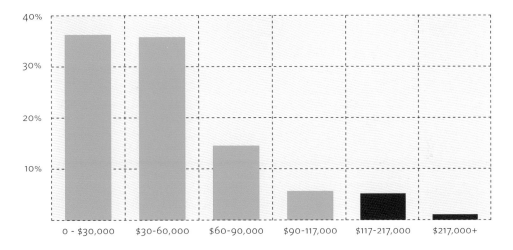

If Social Security covered 90 percent of earnings, only those who earn more than $217,000 would have earnings above the cap.

✦ Revenue increase 3

Tax health insurance

Currently, workers and employers do not pay payroll taxes on compensation in the form of premiums for employer-sponsored health insurance. Repealing this tax preference, gradually over a 10-year period, would significantly broaden the Social Security tax base and increase revenues. This proposal, which has received attention as part of the broader policy debate, would also expand the income tax base.

PROS	CONS
Eliminating the health care tax preference would reduce the 75-year shortfall by about 35 percent.	This policy change, unless paired with an increase in the earnings cap, would not affect higher income taxpayers, whose earnings already exceed the cap.
Eliminating the tax subsidy would raise the cost of health care, which could encourage people to spend less.	Some employers may decide to curtail their health care coverage, so some workers could end up with less-generous plans.

TAX HEALTH CARE PREMIUMS

The health insurance exclusion is the largest preference in the tax code.

↟ Revenue increase 4

Transfer start-up costs to general revenues

Social Security was designed as a self-funding program, with the payroll tax as its dedicated source of revenue. This gives workers the sense that they pay for their own benefits—that Social Security is not a welfare program.

But in the early years of Social Security, retirees got benefits worth far more than what they paid in. The cost of these start-up benefits is now built into the program's ongoing cost.

We could transfer these start-up costs to general government revenues. Then the payroll taxes paid by each generation would closely reflect the benefits it gets.

PROS	CONS
Transferring start-up costs to general revenues solves the 75-year problem.	The transfer would require the federal government to raise taxes and/or cut spending 10 percent.
Getting rid of start-up costs strengthens the link between the taxes each generation pays and the benefits it receives.	Higher income taxpayers, who pay the bulk of federal taxes, could object and withdraw support for the program.

SHIFT THE BURDEN

Should other taxes finance the "start-up" benefits we gave our parents and grandparents?

⬆ Revenue increase

Raise the return on assets

The Social Security Trust Fund currently holds about $2.8 trillion in government bonds. If a portion of these assets were invested in stocks, Social Security could expect to earn a higher annual return, over the long term, on those assets.

To capture these higher returns, one proposal would shift 40 percent of Social Security's assets from bonds to stocks by 2028.

PROS	CONS
Investing 40 percent of Trust Fund assets in equities reduces the 75-year shortfall by about 20 percent.	Stocks are risky. So Social Security would need to adjust benefits or taxes in response to market fluctuations.
It diversifies Social Security's funding base.	Stocks risk government involvement in the economy, which could be limited by capping trust fund holdings and using privately managed index funds.

YIKES!
Stocks promise higher returns, but bring financial and political risks.

↑ Revenue increase [6]

Do nothing (but raise taxes in 2033)

We could do nothing and simply raise the payroll tax when the Trust Fund is depleted. With the Trust Fund gone, Social Security becomes a purely pay-as-you-go program. The payroll tax would need to be 16.2 percent of earnings, split evenly between workers and employers, to pay promised benefits in 2033. By the end of the 75-year time frame, it would need to be 17.3 percent of earnings.

PROS	CONS
Substantially raising the payroll tax to pay benefits when the Trust Fund is depleted solves the problem.	The increase is very large, abrupt, and disruptive.
We don't have to do anything for 20 years.	It could impose significant hardship on low-wage workers, who spend much of their earnings on necessities.

UNPLEASANT SURPRISE

Paying for benefits when the Trust Fund runs dry will take a much larger piece of our earnings.

Taxes as a percent of covered earnings (split evenly between us and our employer) if we do nothing but raise taxes in 2033

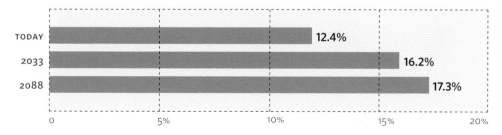

TODAY	12.4%
2033	16.2%
2088	17.3%

0   5%   10%   15%   20%

What about individual accounts?

There are two types of individual accounts. Add-ons require contributions on top of the payroll tax, and do not directly affect Social Security revenues or benefits. Carve-outs let workers send part of their payroll tax to an individual account, which reduces Social Security revenues. But these workers must give up future benefits of equal value, so the shortfall again remains unchanged.

But if the accounts raise retirement incomes, could we cut benefits? Add-ons increase saving and will raise retirement incomes, though by an unknown amount. Carve-outs might raise retirement incomes, but only by accepting more risk. In both cases, the effect on the shortfall is indirect and unclear.

PROS	CONS
Workers could invest in stocks, which have higher expected returns than Social Security.	Stocks are risky, especially for individual investors.
Contributing to such accounts is far more palatable than paying payroll taxes.	Cutting benefits based on the expected returns in individual accounts is risky.
Individual accounts may be a more effective way to build savings than the Trust Fund. This would be so if the government uses Social Security surpluses, lent to the Treasury, to run larger deficits not pay down debt.	Workers with individual accounts might reduce 401(k) or other types of saving, which would offset the positive effect on retirement saving.

NO DIRECT EFFECT

Individual accounts can help only if they increase incomes down the road and allow a cut in benefits.

Time to *fix* the *problem*

A lasting fix would keep Social Security revenues and outlays in balance well beyond the traditional 75-year horizon.

Fixes that balance the books for the next 75 years are not long-lasting if they build up Trust Fund assets in the near term, sell those assets to pay benefits in the out years, and leave the program suddenly short of money when there is nothing left to sell.

A lasting fix could use investment income from the Trust Fund to help pay benefits beyond the 75th year. This approach probably requires the use of equities to boost investment returns. It also requires larger benefit cuts and tax increases than needed in a 75-year fix—to build up a larger Trust Fund and narrow the gap between taxes and benefits. One such fix would raise the payroll tax by 2.9 percent of earnings, index the Full Retirement Age to longevity, and invest 40 percent of Trust Fund assets in equities.

The alternative is to finance benefits beyond the 75th year on a pay-as-you-go basis. We would not need to cut benefits or raise taxes as much in the near term. But at the end of the 75-year horizon, taxes must be 17.3 percent of earnings, benefits 72 cents on the dollar, or some combination of the two.

WHAT MUST BE DONE

*To secure Social Security for our grandchildren's children,
we must build up a much larger Trust Fund or
bequeath much higher taxes or much lower benefits.*

How the proposals stack up

The table lists the contribution each proposal makes toward closing both the 75-year shortfall and the shortfall on the other side of the 75-year horizon. When evaluating the various proposals, note:

1 Benefit cuts lower incomes in retirement. Initiatives that raise revenues primarily lower incomes during our working years.

2 Initiatives that cut benefits generally hit low earners, the disabled, and the oldest old, who are heavily dependent on Social Security. Initiatives that raise revenues primarily hit those with higher incomes.

3 Combining proposals does not reduce the shortfall by the sum of the individual reductions. The effect of changing the Cost-of-Living-Adjustment, for example, falls if we raise the Full Retirement Age.

| | SHORTFALL REDUCTION | |
HOW BENEFITS COULD BE CUT	FOR THE NEXT 75 YEARS	IN THE 75TH YEAR	
Cut benefits today by 17 percent	100%	60%	*pg. 16*
Raise the Full Retirement Age in line with longevity	20%	35%	*pg. 18*
Freeze the purchasing power of benefits	95%	160%	*pg. 20*
Cut benefits for higher earners on a sliding scale	55%	90%	*pg. 22*
Change the Cost-of-Living-Adjustment	20%	15%	*pg. 24*
Do nothing until 2033 (then cut benefits to match tax revenue)	100%	100%	*pg. 26*

HOW REVENUES COULD BE RAISED	FOR THE NEXT 75 YEARS	IN THE 75TH YEAR	
Increase the payroll tax today by 2.9 percent	100%	60%	*pg. 30*
Raise the earnings cap to cover 90 percent of earnings	30%	15%	*pg. 32*
Expand the payroll tax base to include health insurance	35%	20%	*pg. 34*
Use general revenues to finance the legacy debt	100%	100%	*pg. 36*
Invest 40% of Social Security Trust Fund assets in stocks	20%	depends on size of Fund	*pg. 38*
Do nothing until 2033 (then raise taxes to cover benefits)	100%	100%	*pg. 40*

The answers to three key questions will largely determine how we should fix Social Security:

1 Do we want to keep benefits more or less as currently set? If so, how should the burden be shared?

a. By all workers equally, or primarily by those better-off?
b. By workers alone, or by taxpayers generally?

2 Do we want to keep taxes more or less at current levels? If so, how do we cut benefits?

a. Target workers with higher benefits?
b. If we cut across-the-board, how do we assure people that they won't fall into poverty in their old age?

3 Should each generation going forward pay much the same tax and get much the same benefits?

a. This requires the current generation to build up a large Social Security Trust Fund that would probably invest in equities.
b. Or should our children and grandchildren, who will be richer and live longer, pay much more or get a much smaller benefit?

One thing we know for certain. Something will be done in 2033—when Social Security redeems its last bond—unless we do something sooner. And the sooner we act, the easier the fix.

Explanations

Your *Fix-It Book* gets most of its facts and figures from the Social Security Administration. The 2014 Social Security Trustees Report (http://www.ssa.gov/oact/tr/2014/tr2014.pdf) is a basic source. Our "average earner" is its "medium earner;" our "high earner," however, earns nearly twice the medium wage, not 60 percent more. We also rely largely on 2013 estimates of the contribution that reform proposals make to reduce the shortfall, prepared by the Office of the Chief Actuary of the Social Security Administration (www.ssa.gov/oact/solvency/provisions/index.html).

Other facts and figures come from Alicia H. Munnell, *The Declining Role of Social Security* (2003); Congressional Budget Office, *The Distribution of Household Income and Federal Taxes, 2008 and 2009* (2012); and John Geanakoplos, Olivia S. Mitchell, and Stephen P. Zeldes, *Would a Privatized Social Security System Really Pay a Higher Rate of Return?* (1998).

Your authors calculated the benefit of the high earner (p.7); the role of Social Security in the income of the elderly (p.11); the effect of freezing benefits (p.21) and cutting benefits for higher earners by freezing benefits on a sliding scale (p.23); the distribution of earnings in 2012 (p.33); and the effect of transferring start-up costs to the Treasury (p.36). Your authors, of course, accept full responsibility for any and all errors in your *Fix-It Book*.